# POETS FOR PEACE

A COLLECTION

CHAPEL HILL
PRESS, INC.

# POETS FOR PEACE
*a collection*

Compiled and edited by Timothy F. Crowley

COVER IMAGE
The Peace Pole at The North Carolina Botanical Garden in Chapel Hill, NC,
which says "May Peace Prevail on Earth."

"Peace" by William Carlos Williams, from COLLECTED POEMS:
1909-1939, VOLUME I, copyright © 1938 by New Directions
Publishing Corp. Reprinted by permission of
New Directions Publishing Corp. U.S./Canadian rights only.

"Please Call Me By My True Names" and "Peace" reprinted from
*Call Me By My True Names: The Collected Poems of Thich Nhat Hanh* (1999)
by Thich Nhat Hanh with permission of Parallax Press, Berkeley, California.

All proceeds from the sale of this book will be donated to the North Carolina
Poets for Peace Fund, which is dedicated to the cause of promoting world peace.

Published by The Chapel Hill Press, Inc.
600 Franklin Square
1829 East Franklin Street
Chapel Hill, NC 27514

ISBN Number   1-880849-46-1
Library of Congress Catalog   2002101661
Printed in the United States of America

# ACKNOWLEDGMENTS

The majority of the poets who have so generously contributed to this collection are currently residents of North Carolina and are members of the North Carolina Writers' Network, the North Carolina Poetry Society, and the Friday Noon Poets at UNC, or are associated in some way with the Editor. I am most grateful to the following people who have offered their poignant verse as a gift, but are not associated with those organizations:

Ines Arenas Sanchez de Olaya, Colombia, SA
Ed Lyons, Roanoke, VA
William Menza, Fairfax, VA

I thank those poets who have given of themselves without compromise or boundaries and who wish for all of us to share together in the pursuit of world peace:

Joy Acey (Frelinger)
Katherine Russell Barnes
Susan Broili
Sally Buckner
Sheridan Bushnell
Catherine Combs
Bill Coolidge
Kevin Douglas
Gwen Y. Fortune
Janice Moore Fuller
Jaki Shelton Green
Judy Lewis Hench
James Hilden-Minton
Sam R. Hope
Brenda K. Ledford

Mitchell Forrest Lyman
Ed Lyons
David T. Manning
Caroline Rowe Martens
Nannette Swift Melcher
Bonnie Michael
Kym Gordon Moore
Tootsie (Ione) O'Hara
M. L. Parrish
Taylor Reese
Tony Reevy
Victoria Dianne Rende
Patricia Robinson
Lynn Veach Sadler
Linda Salter

Catherine J. Schultz
Joanna Catherine Scott
Ruby B. Shakelford
Doug Stuber
Nancy Simpson
Dianna Smith

Adam Byrne Tritt
Carl Armin Viehe
Richard Alkin Walker
Chris Waters
Eric A. Weil
Carol Williams

The reader should know that the contributing poets are poets-in-residence at universities, college professors, community activists, journalists, published novelists and poets, correctional institution inmates and college students as well as well-versed folks who believe in the written word and its possibilities as a tool for peace.

All earnings from this effort are entering The North Carolina Poets for Peace Fund, a non-profit fund to finance future events furthering the cause of world peace and offering dialogue for completeness.


Thank you,


Timothy F. Crowley
Fellow Poet/Editor

# FOREWORD

Several years ago, I was introduced to the teachings of Buddhist
Master Thich Nhat Hanh. Respectfully referred to as Thây (Teacher),
Thich Nhat Hanh was nominated for the Nobel Peace Prize by Martin
Luther King in 1967. Thây has authored more than thirty-five books
and is a formidable poet as well. For more than forty years, while
living in exile, Thich Nhat Hanh built a community of people of all
races and faiths. He encourages us to follow the best of our spiritual
traditions and work for world peace in order to end the unnecessary
suffering throughout the world.

I have been very much affected by his teachings and, as a result, initi-
ated the following poetic effort more than a year ago. The project took
on a new life following the events of September 11, 2001. Originally
intended to offer a place for North Carolina Writers' Network members
to submit a "Poem For Peace", another dimension surfaced with the
idea that a collection of poems could become a more significant instru-
ment for teaching the concept of peace.

There are many different approaches to poetry within this book. Each
poet strives to provide a stage on which to reach the human soul with
profound simplicity and sophisticated metaphor. All of us struggle
with our demons. Sometimes, for better or worse, it is our demons that
steer our course. I'm trusting *Poets for Peace* will imbue readers with
a sincere energy to reach out to one another. I hope a place for peace
will be found in the hearts and minds of those who read these poems.

Peace has many meanings, among them absence of war, contentment,
and completeness. Poverty and injustice work hand-in-hand opposing
true peace. We can work together to convince others that poverty and
injustice are not necessary for political and social control.

I appealed to poets from the North Carolina Writers' Network family and am most grateful to those who have offered their verse for publication. I thank them for their earnest intentions, and for the kindness and patience that were extended to me. I thank Jaki Shelton Green for her special offering and for inviting me to "give myself permission" to join the world of poets and those who love the written word. I thank Linda Hobson, Director of the NCWN, who encouraged me on the entire journey with this project.

Finally, I thank the Sherman Family—Angela, Nicole, Michael and Robert—who have financially enabled me to pursue *Poets for Peace*.


Timothy F. Crowley

# TABLE OF CONTENTS

# POETS FOR PEACE

## A COLLECTION

Do not say that I'll depart tomorrow
because even today I still arrive.

Look deeply: I arrive in every second
to be a bud on a spring branch,
to be a tiny bird, with wings still fragile,
learning to sing in my new nest,
to be a caterpillar in the heart of flower,
to be a jewel hiding itself in a stone.

I still arrive, in order to laugh and to cry,
in order to fear and to hope,
the rhythm of my heart is the birth and
death of all that are alive.

I am the mayfly metamorphosing
on the surface of the river,
and I am the bird which, when spring comes,
arrives in time to eat the mayfly.

I am the frog swimming happily
in the clear water of a pond,
and I am also the grass-snake who,
approaching in silence,
feeds itself on the frog.

I am the child in Uganda, all skin and bones,
my legs as thin as bamboo sticks,
and I am the arms merchant,
selling deadly weapons to Uganda.

I am the twelve-year-old girl,
refugee on a small boat,
who throws herself into the ocean
after being raped by a sea pirate,
and I am the pirate, my heart not yet capable
of seeing and loving.

I am a member of the politburo,
with plenty of power in my hands,
and I am the man who has to pay his
"debt of blood" to my people,
dying slowly in a forced labor camp.

My joy is like spring, so warm
it makes flowers bloom in all walks of life.
My pain is like a river of tears, so full
it fills up the four oceans.

Please call me by my true names,
so I can hear all my cries and my laughs at once,
so I can see that my joy and pain are one.

Please call me by my true names,
so I can wake up,
and so the door of my heart can be left open,
the door of compassion.


THICH NHAT HANH


3

# ⌒ PEACE ⌒

If you engage with the warrior,
You validate the battle.

If you observe the warrior,
You understand his strategy.

If you hold compassion for the warrior,
You soften the hardness of her heart.

If you love the warrior,
You melt it.


SHERIDAN BUSHNELL

The airplane lifts
toward the west.
I raise a magazine
to read but can't

turn from the cover,
a photo of a face
skin tight over skull
lips dry, eyes dull

from a hunger traveling
person to person,
a message burning
in empty bellies.

Fingers thin as strings
hold onto hope for food.
Moons of dark thirst,
stare across miles of ocean.

The pilot's voice announces
*We're over Oklahoma.*
I know below are rivers,
fields of wheat and cattle.

Flight attendants roll carts
canned juices, sodas
peanuts in foil wrappers
ask what I'd like to have.

IONE (TOOTSIE) O'HARA

# ⌇ MASS GRAVE(S) ⌇

I, Klis Senj, the Uskok,
hate Turks and Austrians.
But most — Venetians — vain and venomous.

In Dalmatia, we Uskoks
fled before Ottoman hordes.
We were Uskoci — "The Fugitives."
We made our stand near Split
in the Fortress Klis
We fought the Turks five years,
for so it pleased the Venetians until
they signed a pact with Turks
and made us Uskoci go.

We settled at Senj, north of Zadar,
learned to make the lightest,
fastest ships anyone had seen,
boats built to fit our Dalmatian coast.
We used them to harass every Turkish ship.
Strip and sink that Turkish ship! Strip and sink!
Oh, but that revenge was sweet.
The Venetians and the Catholic Church?
They aided and abetted, urged us Uskoci on.
For close to thirty years,
we bled Turkish ships —
and Turkish ships alone!
We were no pirates.
We were privateers.
Like the British Drake and Morgan.

Then Venice flew its
skull and crossbones yet again,
made peace with the Ottomans,
made Uskoks outcasts once more.
Neither Great Venice nor Great Austria
would let us re-settle on farmland.

We had no choice:
Uskoks became well and truly pirates,
Venetian ships our favorite plunder.
When Venetians captured us Uskoks,
their tortures were ungodly.
Then they blockaded Senj,
tried to starve us Uskoks out.
They could not stop us being still
a starving dog after Venetian bones.
Many outside heard our story,
thought us right — courageous.
Noblemen, adventurers, and more outcasts
like us joined our cause
to live gloriously on borrowed time.

Venice was well and truly courtesan again,
feigned to go to war with Austria
over us Uskoks.
In their so-called treaty, Austria agreed
"to liquidate the Uskok pirates' nest."
They hanged, beheaded till they tired,
then said they were transporting

the remains of us Uskoks to a place interior—
which is all that we had ever asked.
It was given out that we had been deported
to pretty villages in the Krajina.
No trace of us Uskoks was ever found.

I, Klis Senj, the Uskok,
preserve Uskoci history
in my name.
I have ventured forth
through centuries
to chant this slaughter song
upon our very abattoir
enticing investigators of today's mass grave
to dig deeper, to discover
what befell us Uskoks.

LYNN VEACH SADLER

I lean against the columns left,
lain to trace the echoes
lost from marble leaf.

Beneath me olives' silver waves
fragment the edge of waters,
limpid, summerstill.

Faint scent of eucalyptus wafts,
and redolence of thyme
off the rugged hills.

Other supplicants thread their way
up the ancient trail.
Was any born to peace?

M. L. PARRISH

# CHAINS

The sharp cry of a baby
Carries down through the ghetto.

Stolen goods clank
Inside the shoulder bags
Of children not yet teens—

Children scrounging the streets
For something     anything
That can be turned into

*White powder or liquid death.*

They hear the cries
And pity the tiny babe,
Knowing what his life will be like

Here, where darkness falls
Even in the daylight...

*Here, where there is no escape,*
*Where chains are not*
*What takes the prisoner.*

VICTORIA DIANNE RENDE

3.19.99

I grant you: peace is desirable. War being, in a figure,
its antithesis is wholly detestable to the lover of peace.

But there are lovers and lovers.

It is stupid to advocate peace in order to have me work
in a factory or a field or a mine or a quarry or a forest
or on the sea or at a desk or on the ice or at the sea's bottom—
unless I please to do these things.

To substitute for me a lesser war for another greater
is the hollowest mockery—to substitute war with fire by
war with mud is vilest deception.
Either I must have war or none.

Peace is noble only when it sends me out a tramp—
my peace made with the world—
a lily of the field if you will.

But who is there that advocates peace? I have seen
no true apostles. I have read of few. And it is notable
that these do not form societies — Tolstoi to the contrary.

Peace requires genius to be preached. It is a rare
high thing—it is not subsidized—it also has its courage.

WILLIAM CARLOS WILLIAMS

She was cold, you understand.
My desire
was to take her by the hand,
to lead her to  someplace warm.
I had seen her the day before
at a rally,
in protest of the war
and was taken.
Really,
I was shaken
by her beauty and her poise.
I spoke to her below the noise.
"Excuse me," I said, "I don't mean to bother
but I just wanted to tell you
you're simply so ... incredibly beautiful.
I'm glad you're here."
I swallowed my fear and put my hand on her shoulder
surprised at what I had told her.
She said thank you
and smiled
so complete
and sweet a smiling face
that in that moment
there was love
and grace.

We held a vigil in the freezing night.
We somehow thought it only right
to come and pray
and stay
and light candles
drawing wax pictures on the cement:
a civil show of our dissent.

The blankets long had been unrolled
and coffee poured against the cold.
Hands warmed through paper cups.
Chants to keep the spirit up.
Some had huddled against the wind
that wouldn't cease
and the bitter chill,
their only protection a sturdy will
and a burning devotion to peace.

Then I saw in the numbing air
a shivering figure with long black hair
committed or stupid, or so bold
as to come without a coat into the cold.

ADAM BYRN TRITT

## ☞ BALLADE FOR OUR LADY ☜

Mother, we have no frankincense or myrrh
to set before you on your hill.
Peace in our time is just a blur,
a distant make-believe until
you pray for us. Because you will,
we tape upon your plaster crease
our humble gold, this dollar bill.
Eternal Mary, grant us peace.

Mild Mary, if we often err
our prayers are no less strong. You fill
our sinful hearts with hope. Deter
our brother-killing ways, distill
love from our glory songs, instill
wisdom in us, grant us a lease
on constant peace. We know you will.
Eternal Mary, grant us peace.

Madonna, help us not prefer
these words to sense. We mustn't spill
the blood of Abel, must bestir
ourselves to action, learn the skill
of peace, by our own wits must still
the madness, giving you surcease
for lesser intercessions. Still,
Eternal Mary, grant us peace.


ENVOI


Lady, we pray you on your hill
In human hearts to bring release
From human suicidal will.
Eternal Mary, grant us peace.


CHRIS WATERS

Is this an unplanned rose from
our backyard
sticking out her tongue
in anger, in tease, in trust
of a medicine man?

Is this post-explosion of bloom
a petal awaiting its descent
to earth? Surrounded by
colors, converting from green to
red, to spotted tan?
Is that a Man with a Gun?

How often within this season
do we have this scene within
our sight and not see it?
With a flicker with a finger on a
trigger, we can start downward
all over again!

Let's see if this child can.
Let's see if this child can smile.
Let's see if this child can smile
once more.

Is it not possible to change
as the seasons?
Can we start once again?
Or is it just a flower?

TIMOTHY F CROWLEY

Far away from the world,
a holy hush fills the hills-
a temple beneath silken skies
where I find peace in the storm.

Fields swell with goldenrod
and dogwoods wear crosses,
a Monarch butterfly casts
a shadow on scorched grass.

Poplar leaves rustle
in the rasping wind.
Warning posted on the coast-
a mean season for hurricanes.

Global warming, school violence,
fires raging out west.
A bomb slaughters children:
the world shatters my tranquility.

BRENDA KAY LEDFORD

## THE SEARCH

I ran with men up Bunker Hill;
The fires of Gettysburg
Are with me still.
I rode with Custer o'er the plain,
Looked down on San Juan Hill.
I've searched for peace,
Abiding peace,
Yet it escapes me still.

I loved both sides at Chateau Thierry
And crossed Remagen Bridge.
I swam the Yalu in Korea,
Saw Saigon behind a hedge.

I've searched for peace
In every battle
I've heard bold statesmen's
Idle prattle.

Yet peace is still an idle word,
Through atom bomb it can't be heard.
Must fiery death
The world ignite
E're yet this globe
Is set aright?

A child cries,
A mother moans
I look and there
Another groans.

O God, where is this thing called peace
That humankind may find release?
Must nuclear bomb
And Star wars, too
Reduce this sphere
To ash and glue?

I stand before the Lord and cry
"Don't let all human beings die."
He spoke to me, "Let justice roll;
My will shall rest upon your soul."

"Go forth once more
To humankind
To plead for peace
Peace you shall find."

So here I stand upon the shore,
Yon mountain's heights
And ocean's roar,
It's peace at last
I've found surcease
Where men from war
Will grant release.

Then quiet reigns
And all is still
As I look out
From my Spirit hill.

CARL ARMIN VIEHE

Standing by Lincoln,
the angel of our better selves looked on,
while the crack burst onto the stage,
piercing the peace that might have been.
I wonder if he pined to trip the light fantastic,
or dance an earthy jig, as both exited the theatre.
Perhaps a tasty kiss or a shiver up the spine
trembled parched lips and pounded a heart long since gone.
Maybe visions of riding in a Dallas motorcade, the destination true, amused him,
as he observed the firing bursts of quanta shape-shift from waveform to particle.
Did he debate time the component of intention or intention as unconscious outcome.
Eons of waiting the incredulity of the very moment,
may have transfixed him,
may have diverted him,
may have made peace the handmaiden of time.


CATHERINE COMBS

## ⌐ PROPHECY ⌐

These seem
the best days,

the water clear,
just chilling.

Rippled by minnows.

Above the stream,
mountains march
in a line like giants.

At the tree line,
what stirs,

what black
shape rises

to scatter
sunning cougars,

to rout even
the old ones,
watching over the people,
from ancient hills?

Seek the cars, the
houses, the
rising dust
behind your wheels—

it does not suffice.

TONY REEVY
SEPTEMBER 9,2001

Brushed by sidhe spirit,
Wistful winds skirt silent streams.
Matador, gladiator, pugilist.
Abandoned by entire entourage
Countering deep
For Olympian courage.

Beast, braggart, jester
Disloyal to the kingdom.
Unresponsive to the palace
As War finds a fellow Enemy
Displacing funds for
A never ending other
War-Poverty.

Overused god enters again and again
Placing Race in the Face of mediocre
Men. A breeze before the storm.
Van Rosenveldt, O'Cruadhlaoich, Smith,
Cabotini, Clay, Wayne
Cursed for changing allegiance to a foreign god
And from a slave-given name.
The voice for an age; a messenger
Whispering, screaming defiance.
Jabbing at Death, crushing shame.

Bearer of Olympian myth
Stripped clean.
Gory Glory, Peace, Everything
Not bearing false witness to
Those who
Undermined him. We're one, two,
Free. Co-existing Truth
and Spirit of Dignity...
Spirit of ancestry
Living the Persona
Breaking doors for Liberty

...

Ali...

TIMOTHY F. CROWLEY

Breathless at this time,
humanity awaits the future.
Where will it be a century
from  today?

This world rumbles,
offers no real solutions—
At least permanent and
positive ones.

Using power and intimidation,
its actions unravel the lands of time,
Without accepting that neither are answers,
just prolongations of anxiety and greed.

Perhaps it is so written,
and little can be done,
As the past has yet to teach us how
to solve humanity's thirst for peace.

TAYLOR REESE

# THERE WAS NOTHING WE COULD DO

We felt it, even in the place we are—
to us the terrorist also left a scar.

We watched in amazement as part of our America fell—
as we did, it gave us quite a story to tell.

We watched Americans shocked, literally in a daze—
as they screamed and ran from the deadly haze.

It was hard watching as fellow Americans
picked their own time to die—
as they tried their best to show courage,
as they jumped the world watched and cried.

We felt so helpless watching what America was going through—.
what makes it hurt even worse, because we were prisoners;
there was nothing we could do.

PATRICIA ROBINSON
9-12-01- 9:00

Walking the shore, meeting place of life
amid life, with the resulting detritus
of daily battles scattered about,
I watch a gull attack a crab
beneath a sky as blue as anyone
might desire for a last glimpse of this world.
Eye to eye, the gull feints a jab,

the crab holds claws up like a basketball
player defending the lane. Black eye
in a cocked, gray-feathered head, beak
a hooked blade, a lever, a quick flick
of the neck to click on the reddish shell
and the large claw hammering the beak.
Flipped, the crab lands cat-like,

extends open pincers, still
as waiting traps, a dare. The battleground,
the sand, the incessant wave-sound
and uncountable shells and pieces
of shells of clam and cochina
and crab and whelk. I approach
the stand-off, the bird flaps, gives ground.

Crouching, I see it's a she-crab,
her belly covered with eggs
in their slick jelly, eggs as black
as two hundred gulls' eyes. Inclined
to walk a spectator's distance
and let nature battle nature
for survival, Thoreau's ants in mind,

I relent, as random shell-bits
remind me of a news photo:
a human skull on its side in the mud
of Rwanda or Kosovo,
unidentifiable beyond
the certain suffering, and I keep
the gull away. But the she-crab won't go

into the waves and safety. Despite
my shooing and splashing, she, armored knight
with upstretched sword and shield, defends
her innocent brood against me. That
mud-slick skull — chosen from a crowd,
perhaps he saw a sky like this one
before the machete or the bullet,

perhaps he died knowing some revenge;
his pregnant wife had crossed
the border. Finally, I pick up
a sandy disk of crabshell, debris
of an earlier seagull supper,
thrust it at the larger claw. She
clamps it and I carry her

to the lapping water, where
she scuttles into the breakers, waving
her cousin's carapace overhead,
I don't know whether in thanks
or defiance, while the gull
glides above the foam, this failure
forgotten in the search for another meal.

ERIC A. WEIL

Guitar, mandolin, violin and banjo
in the second row, drums,
smiles on all their faces.
A spirit of enthusia envelops this crowd.

This spirit, it's adrift,
springing on me visiting Boulder,
place of my first academic failing,
this return, some decades later, I wonder if
my search for companion, for love
is finally acquitted?

I sit on this old wooden,
paint-scarred stool
strobe lights above me
heating my head while
lighting up the stage.

The spirit has moved on to a nearby table.
It washes over two men,
who appear, like my daughter Molly,
to live in a group home.

Out for the night, with two chaperones,
Or house managers, four to a table.
These two guys sit, eyes glued
On the band.

One of the chaperones leaves,
returns with two long necked root beers.
These two swig, like my older
brothers taught me.

Lift high the bottle
Drain a few ounces then
bring it down fast,
curtailing any foam.

These two guys do that,
perfect grins appearing behind upraised bottles
then "WHACK!" bottles on wood table,
like the wild flap of a beaver tail on stilled water
Now their hands, on the table, clutching
the brown glass, never out of reach.

I want to sit at their table
Smile and laugh as they do
Drink a long-necked root beer
Grins shared with affection,
a sign of gratitude
For friends and root beer, music
A night out on the town.

The stool I'm sitting on
is near the cash register.
People bump into me
as they line up to order and pick up.

Like a sailboat teetering
with gusty wind, they move
between tables and me,
off-balance, so touch is necessary.
I smile. Most everyone returns my smile.

This solitude is like going to the basement
and discovering a hothouse of plants
all the colors of a rainbow.

Some days, not so long ago
the house of my mind would get
so small, I'd be smothered, deadended
so I'd take to the water.

Last week, on the bay
An old man fishing
on the dock with two boys
speaking Spanish watch me loft my boat.
"Que es eso?" I mimic rowing, asking
for the word..."rameer", they shout in
unison. I smile. The old man
chuckles. No fish caught.

So many ways to eat
myself up from the inside
hardly any way
not to go for the bait.

Maybe what I've wanted
is not only what I'm not getting
but also what I don't need.

Maybe it's occasional
surprising interactions like this
which tip the balance.

Dogs, birds, sealife. I've become
a solitary lover.
I'm being fashioned in some new way.

But at the Twisted Vine bar, so content
was I, discovering within me
a hothouse basement,
steaming, not dark at all.


BILL COOLIDGE

What kind of peace for all,
To watch a rose unfold, in budding charm,
Fingers push to a warming soil,
Hands feel a toiling peace,

Rain soaking barren earth,
Returns again, a drenching peace,
Winds skip over land and sea,
A roaring or whispering kind of peace,

Unmatched others meet like the wind,
Freely moving from place to place,
Love's momentum spreads,
In its own timeless space,

The wind, the rain, the sun,
Make rest and endless mating peace,
In minds and tender souls,
Landlings of a world peace,

Let's join the wind, the rain, the sun,
All find lasting peace, from above,
Forever blending as just one,
Like the wind, the rain, the sun.

CAROL WILLIAMS

It was always a fragile dream
this peace,
written in disappearing ink
fading hour by hour
while we watched
in mild dismay.

Now the words are invisible
gone
while we shopped
and cooked
and watered the flowers
and didn't look.

But there are ways
to make the invisible
visible
spin a new dream
resilient
not so prone
to disappear.


BONNIE MICHAEL

# ⌒ SWEETHEART ⌒

I hold you in my hands
in front of the mirror
of my mind.
"You're kind to me".


What do you wish
with this intensity?
To reproduce another you,
seeking eternity?
Hold me calmly in your hands
in front of the mirror
of your mind.


Am I the hunted?
Are you the hunter?
Am I some fear-filled fantasy?
Can we coexist as one,
extending kindness to our other being,
planning and planting
harmoniously?


Misuse of all natural resources
requires we plan and plant as one.
With equanimity...
hold me in your hands
in front of the mirror
Of our mind — peacefully.

Let us massage away
these layers of mistrust, cynicism
and disrespect.
Allow these hands
and heart and mirror of the mind
to be one?

Hold me in your heart
in front of  the mirror
of your mind.


TIMOTHY F. CROWLEY

## WHAT REMAINS?

There was an explosion
in the collective consciousness
of humanity

Images of unspeakable horror
instantly relayed and re-relayed
over and over again

Being everywhere
at Once.

At once, there was
the terror of death approaching
as the plane is about to crash ...

At once, there was
the justification and steadfast commitment
to a cause known only to the heavens ...

At once, there were flames
everywhere and smoke and soot
and shock and instinctual self-preservation...RUN!

At once, there was selfless courage
adrenalin surging, unwavering determination
to save as many as possible
help as many as possible

At once,
there was pitch darkness

At once, there was an overwhelming recognition
of the preciousness of Life
and, in particular, the preciousness of loved ones
and the need to tell them so
be it from an airplane, or an 82nd floor
or a farm in Kansas City, or an apartment in Chicago or ...

At once, there was uncontrollable sobbing
and the pain of irreparable loss
and the fear of irreparable repercussions ...
At once, there was
blinding rage and hatred
and the need to "do something"
to squelch this open, hemorrhaging wound
be it through accusations, violence, money, blood ...

At once, there was silent order
collective movement
the presence of peace
stillness, grace
overwhelming love
apparent as the mind stilted, halted
its normal routine from shock and disbelief ...

The unbelievable had occurred.

The unthinkable was witnessed fully.

Now
what is unthinkable
is all that is present
all that remains

Let not the mind begin its routine again
Let not the dead and the living be disturbed
Instead a re-minder


Silence and presence remain
because they are unthinkable

Let these that prevail hold
lay bare, embrace
this opportunity
to rest in this peace
that remains

Everywhere at Once


CATHERINE J. SCHULTZ, PH. D.

# ☞ PEACE ☜

To me peace should be in the heart.

To a soldier who has gone to another country
to fight for the land he loves, and took the pledge
for honor and valor.
With all the love he had for his family
He still had to depart.
But now I am waiting for some peace to come in
my heart.
I lost someone I truly loved this year.
And it's really more than I can bear.
Everyone says it will be okay,
But I'm still anticipating the coming of that day.
I know God has the answers,
and golden keys.
Maybe one day he will give me the peace and love
I need.

LINDA D. SALTER

6.11.01

Symbols succumb to inevitable
Demons, dramatically diminishing the possible.
An Autumn pond reflects
Change in the air.
Solemnity, lethargy, sadness, despair
Clouds of warning
An Indian Summer storm
Disperses dreaming with
A clash of forces
About to meet head on.

Again and again and again
And again...
Man's reptilian answer to life's task
Strike an innocent citizen neighbor, then ask
For the answer to the wounded prayer.
Force, Oh force. A false piece unto itself.
Boundaries, territories, belief systems, truths
Ingredients blended as unbaked pastry pieces.
When will it correct itself as simply as
The seasons??

How can we capture completeness??

TIMOTHY F. CROWLEY
9.16.01

How do you develop joyful calmness,
The serenity of a stable mind
That's centered in a peaceful place
With who you are and what you are
And think and say and do each day;
And during those long nights
Of this and that anxiety or sorrow.

I've heard ancient masters say:
Move toward the sharp points.
See all as teachers, medicine.
See all as enlightened wisdom.
Be with the earth, the blue sky,
A singing bird, yourself,
Just as they are
in perfect perfection.

WILLIAM MENZA
FEBRUARY 14, 2000

We parked on pavement behind Suder School,
walked down a dense trail
away from the sound of traffic, back,
back one hundred twenty-seven years

into a Georgia wood thicket of 1864.
We walked right through the middle
of a Confederate bivouac with low tents
and men roasting corn over a campfire.

They did not look at us, though,
we were close enough to touch,
near enough to hear the man
cleaning his rifle say—

*Buddy, It'll kick.*
*You've gotta aim low.*
*Aim for the kneecap,*
*Hit him in the chest.*

They seemed to be ghost soldiers
trapped in time. We felt trapped too
on a red dirt road, crowded with travelers —
refugees and people like us who came to see.

We passed breastworks and men behind them,
crouched, quaint as figments in a dream.
In a stir of dust beside the road,
we watched Union troops drill — *Forward. Step Four.*

A roar went out through the crowd
and the whisper — *Atlanta is lost at Jonesboro.*
Drums sounded nearer and we saw movement
through the dappled woods. Soldiers marched

from three directions onto the open field
and with the bugle call, they charged.
When we heard the boom of cannons,
the clack of gunfire and saw men falling,

writhing in the dirt, we could do nothing
but fall to the ground ourselves,
pull our frightened children close to us
and watch soldiers kill each other again.


NANCY SIMPSON

I.

Hand over hand we move
bucket, a brigade of living work.
Our hands touch, span in a bridge
of moving plastic pails. Filled
with soft gray ash
a sooty cement substance
grit, remains from
twin towers of strength.

II.

At the head of the line, Carlos
wears a surgical mask.
Small protection for his lungs —
singe, smoke, asbestos
still cling to the vapor.

He scoops, shovels
full of detritus
into the plastic pails,
three scoops fill it.
Three scoops enough
to pass it
through the hands
to a waiting diesel
dump truck —
the engine running.

Scoop, scoop, scoop
shovel full after shovel full
all day long
all night long.
The only reality is in the rhythm
the routine of repetition.
Someone yells.
All work stops.
While everyone listens
all hands hopeful.
A dog yelps.
A horn blast
false alarm
and we move again.
Set our rhythm.
Scoop, scoop, scoop.
Hand to hand combat with
these twin showers of strength.

III.

The hours wear
we all wearily work.
The soot becomes its own
personality. Carlos makes out
pieces of a puzzle
in his
scoop, scoop, scoop.

That small piece of paper
is a cell from the picture
Donna's six-year-old daughter
drew for Mommy to tape
on her wall.

There is sinew
of mirror David checked
in the men's room
each morning to see
that his tie was straight.

This scoop is tendons
of the school photograph
showing Colin, the beloved
son, of Marta the receptionist.

That melted gray plastic lump
is bones from Ravi's keyboard.
This scoop has muscled wads like the ones
Kami and Steve used to throw
over their cubicle divider
when they talked on the phone.
Here is blood of blue metal from that divider.
This shovel fills with the throb of charred papers
from Harvey's in box.
All those lives came tumbling down
in less than our
twin hours of strength.

IV.

The bucket blisters get bigger
but no one complains.
We are fighting for
twin powers and strength.
God, please help us
in these dark hours.
Give us the strength.


JOY ACEY (FRELINGER)

The children showed us the snake
in a box. "He's pretty,"
they cried. "May we keep him?"

"Are you sure he can't get out?"

"I'm sure," the wisest one said.
"When you get used to him,
we'll let him go free."

But he could get out — and did.
The children were gone, and we
were far from used to him!
A snake loose in the garden!
What we knew of snakes was to
fear them, hate them.

The cat showed us where
he was hiding.
Emotion erupted complete.
The children returned. Would
not hear our pleas.
"You killed him," they screamed.
"He was not harmful, but helpful.
Would keep our garden free of pests,
and he had no poison at all."

How could they know
that opinions long held
are slow to let go?

KATHERINE RUSSELL BARNES

They woke me this morning
To tell me my brother had been killed in battle.
Yet in the garden, uncurling moist petals,
A new rose blooms on the bush.
And I am alive, can still breathe the fragrance of roses and dung,
Eat, pray and sleep.
But when can I break my long silence?
When can I speak the unuttered words that are choking me?


THICH NHAT HANH
1967

La noche esta oscura y dormida,
susurra entre los árboles el viento
trayendonos aroma de plantas floridas
y una voz lejana narra un cuento.

Hoy como ayer la noche es plácida,
nada hace pensar en terrible tormenta,
tormenta de guerra fratricida
que a todos por igual nos atormenta.

Oh Dios! Apiadate; el mundo te lo implora
caen los niños inocentes
ensangrentadas sus hermosas frentes
y por sus hijos toda madre llora.

INES ARENAS SANCHEZ DE OLAYA

This night is dark and asleep,
the wind whispers between the trees,
carrying the aroma of floral plants
and a distant voice narrates a story.

Today, as yesterday, the night is calm,
there are no thoughts of a horrid storm,
the storm of fratricidal war
that torments us all the same.

Oh God! Take pity on us: The world implores you.
Innocent children fall
with blood on their beautiful foreheads
and for our children, all mothers cry.

INES ARENAS SANCHEZ DE OLAYA

People are gone
but their dreams are still here.
They drift in dust and smoke
where crashing towers
became a tomb.
Hanging in haze over
a shattered fortress
nest in autumn trees
above scarred earth

Small dreams:
backyard picnics.
A walk
by the sea
A loved one's embrace.

Large dreams,
dreams of Peace, Justice
and Freedom.
We who remain
may claim these dreams
support them, protect them
nurture them,
try
to bring sanity back
to the world.

NANNETTE SWIFT MELCHER

Eyes of an old man
in the face of a boy
gaze from a broken window
on a world gone awry in Sarajevo.
Life is a flicker,
death, an unwelcome playmate,
for the child in the window.

Yet amid the rubble and despair,
away from sniper's fire,
two boys play a game of catch.
Their eyes, the eyes of children,
their laughter chases death,
for a sliver of time,
in a pock-marked alley of hope.

DIANA SMITH

# ARMISTICE IS ONLY WORDS AWAY

Red and yellow leaves smash above remaining green
On brittle trees stressed by drought.
The fall crop grows together from fear.
War ruins the party here, starving refugees move out.

Warm sun parches grass to dust in Chapel Hill.
Light kills. News disrupts gentle walks.
Two thousand one claims close lives, no way to hide
The reign death's image starts with superficial talk.

Peaceful winds entice lovers bent on keeping war at bay.
Rice is blown to bits, extreme starvation, war means war.
The dissidents' Gulag hut awaits activist Americans,
And your flag decal won't get you into heaven anymore.

Three deer caught in lights that look like monster's eyes.
Nature, fraught with tarmac, endures another "bombs away."
Scream young angst poets. Wipe the cynical smirk off and scream!
One life to infect your neighborhood. One chance only: today.


DOUG STUBER

What heartache do you try to hide
behind remarks you make so snide?
I try to reach out as a friend,
but you go straight off the deep end.
Who hurt you so that you can't heal?
Who caused the agony I can see that you feel?
I know that I can do without
the defensive words you always shout.
But you'll come back, you always do,
because you know I offer friendship that is true.
All I ask is to let me speak,
without the havoc your shouting will wreak.
Let your noble side overrule the other,
so we can commune as brother to brother.
We won't always agree, but try to understand,
we each have a part in God's greater plan.
Let's join together and work toward peace.
Maybe we can do more, but at the very least-
let's talk about our differences, man to man,
and build us a bridge to cross the span.
For peace begins with you and me,
it is only with peace that we will all be free.

RICHARD ALLEN WALTER
(10 NOVEMBER 2001 0854 HOURS)

## ⌒ THE WILD ROSE ⌐

Those were better days.
The rose bloomed on a wild hilltop
Near where the town's main street became a country road.
In those days, hikers climbing there
Smelled the musk of its blood-red flowers,
And painters came to paint
The points of sunlight playing on its leaves.

On a warm afternoon in August,
The townspeople gathered on a field at the foot of the hill.
A band played songs they all knew by heart,
On the grass they ate sandwiches and drank beer from bottles,
On the grass their children played tug-of-war and blind man's bluff.
That evening when lovers walked quietly away to the rose on the hilltop
And the others walked home,
They all thought the vague sadness they felt
Was from being tired out after a long day in the sun.

In the middle of the night,
Something went wrong. By morning
Banners lined the streets, and posters
Of a shadowy enemy with fixed bayonet covered
The walls of the public buildings.
Soon conscripts bivouacked on the hill
Saw the rose's dun and brittle leaves drop,
And women from the brothels watched its blossoms blacken.

It is late November.
Jagged clouds cover the sky. They will snow.
The geese have gone far south.
The rose's thorns lie snarled on the hillside
Like barbed wire across battlefields.
The wind drones like a sullen motor.
A pale red glowing grows in the east.
In the bitter cold of winter,
The bombers will come, and after them the big guns.


ED LYONS

Fluidly cascading in global dimensions
the faces,
like Autumn's tapestry,
are multitextural, multicolored and multifaceted.

Dialects meander
through the natural terrain
with a melody that resonates
like classical sheet music for a piano recital.

As trees, planted by still waters,
clusters of integrated nationalities whisper
theatrical compositions
of robust flavors.

Though many weeds exist to defy freedom,
happiness and the commonwealth,
metamorphosis remains
an inevitable component.

Seedlings fall upon the fertile lands
sprouting new legacies of their ancestry;
if the byproduct of evil prevails,
goodness shall triumph and reign.

This symphony of cultural tapestry
woven for eternal coexistence,
framed under a celestial umbrella
reaches beyond all frontiers.

Faith germinates hope
prayer fertilizes deliverance
understanding irrigates growth
mercy harvests peace.

KYM GORDON MOORE

Prula, age three, was captured
to be bride by brothers
from the other side of the sacred mountain

Too soon, memories are lost
of Mother, Father and clan
who migrate on glacial lakes.

Laughing boys in loose jeans,
girls too young for bras,
re-create an ancient battle
in a "homeland" they've never seen.

The teacher asks, "*In event of war
between this place and that
for which would you fight?*"

Eyes wide, their lips tight,
with a single voice the children cry,
*That place.*

Fright harbors in hyphenated names;
isolation is primal hubris!
ages pass, the beat remains.
What flag will wave,
what anthem blare,
what bands      what drums?
Will Prula forget, forgive,
Or always remember?

GWEN Y. FORTUNE
CONCEIVED DURING THE WAR BETWEEN ISRAEL AND PALESTINE IN 1967

Across the wide Atlantic,
and many decades,
grey waters surge.

Here, just off the Carolina coast,
beneath noon skies, a crewman tallies
vehicles on the deck of the Hatteras ferry,
checks the heavy chocks blocking tires
of the sleek RV at the rear; his companion stretches
the steel chain, tests its clasps, nods.
No need for words.

> *No permission for words;*
> *words are dangerous — "loose lips sink ships" —*
> *wordlessly, the commander lifts his hand,*
> *and the landing craft moves into the channel,*
> *churning pre-dawn waters.*

Behind the ferry
a frothy wake fascinates the children —
lots of children, dressed in cheerful shirts
and bright shorts; some dare to lean
over the rail, others hold tight
to their parents' hands.

> *Lots of barely-bearded*
> *boys hold tight to cherished parents' pictures,*
> *or those of wives or infants, or medallions*
> *bearing the likeness of Christ or St. Christopher.*
> *Some whisper prayers; some contrive jokes,*
> *then stifle nervous laughter, lest it echoes*
> *signal waiting ears on the Normandy shore.*

On the Hatteras shore, patient vacationers
guard fishing lines, watch for telltale bobbles.
Nearby a graceful squadron of pelicans,
fourteen in all, glide and swerve, inches
above the inlet's gleaming surface.
   *Squadrons*
  *of planes, far beyond counting, blacken*
  *the night sky further, their ferocious roar*
  *providing prelude to the fierce staccato*
  *of artillery fire raining the Normandy coast*
  *from the armada that stretches to the horizon.*


Lining the ferry rail, suntanned tourists
armed with camera and camcorder
shoot onto film the fishers on the shore,
the bare ribs of cottages-to-be,
a yacht off starboard, flags cheerily saluting.
  *No flags visible in slate-gray channel air,*
  *but clusters of bright shellbursts accompanied by*
  *the clamor of guns speaking their unspeakable language.*

Above the ferry, white gulls clutter the air,
squabble, and complain to passengers.
To the east, in serene blue skies,
great white clouds swell and billow.
  *Still further east, against night skies*
  *white parachutes swell and billow;*
  *hundreds of men with blackened faces*
  *drop silently into alien land.*

The ferry eases into port; chains fall,
passengers board luggage-crammed vehicles,
gun motors, then, given the signal,
lurch to the quiet shore of Ocracoke.

> *The landing craft lowers its steel ramp;*
> *soldiers hoist seventy-five pound burdens,*
> *move forward, step chin-deep into icy waters*
> *and a burning barrage of bullets.*

Eight miles down Ocracoke, a grizzled grandpa
hoists his wriggling grandson to his shoulder,
points to the shaggy ponies grazing
in their fenced refuge.

At this moment,
beyond Omaha Beach, a man kneels
before one of nine thousand crosses,
bows his white head. His wife kneels beside him,
rubs his shoulder. Pain, securely stowed
for fifty years, leaks from his eyes, his pores.
His fingers reach to touch the name. They tremble.

And grey waters surge.

SALLY BUCKNER

I watched two boys
In the yard from my window.
The big white boy
Shoving his shoulder
Into the chest of the black.

"What's goin' on out there?"
I yelled.

The anger just being born
Died at the sound of a voice.

There was a moment
Of startled guilt.
Then the black boy defended
The bully. "We wuz jus' playin.'"
"He tole me a button
was gone off'n
my jacket."

RUBY P. SHACKELFORD

*"Oh, love let us be true*
*to one another!*
.....................................

*And, we are here as on a darkling plain*
*Swept with confused alarms of struggle and flight*
*Where ignorant armies clash by night."*

MATTHEW ARNOLD, "DOVER BEACH"

*"Owls hoot to mark their territory; whistling is a contact call."*

DUNCAN BROWN, WELSH NATURALIST

We gather near Afon Dwyfor at the moth trap
to see what the blue light has drawn to it in the dark.
What we call a moth, Duncan tells us,
is just one stage, the imago,
the final flowering of its univoltine life.
He scoops out each one, careful not to crimp a wing,
speaks its poet's name before freeing it,
small phoenix, common marble carpet,
Svenson's copper underwing, pink bardsallo.
The Latin names, he says, echo evolutionary orders,
categories constantly changing.

These days, nations seal their borders,
rage the enemy's name in a clear taxonomy —
Israel, India, Palestine, Afghanistan, America, Uzbekistan,
forgetting how identities can blur.
When Tomahawk missiles gather, when six-shooters
slip from their holsters, what hope
even for lovers, like you and me?
Shell-shocked by old partings
how can we hope to lay aside our weapons —
the gunmetal silence, the empty e-mail screen.

Peter Howson's "The Morning After"
monoprint and oil on paper:
A couple parted after sex,
the female amassed inert on the edge
of the bed, back turned like a shield.
Her mate, escaped from the other side,
hunches over, mouth wrenched wide
to regurgitate a scream.
A hand, no longer his,
claws the air above his head.
Blood shadows the front of him.
His or hers? Impossible to say.
His soft genitals surface in the Venice red.
Outside the window, a wide-bodied plane
hovers above a building only six stories high,
a patient lover stroking with its wing.

Duncan says most creatures mark their domains.
Owls hoot and swoop along the edge of night.
Even moths claim their spots of light.

Tonight when we flutter together in the dark,
no taxonomies, please. Call me Yellow Brimstone.
I'll name you July Highflier.
*Melyn y drain, esgynnwr Gorffenaf.*
Then watch while I trace a circle
of candlelight on the bed,
and, for this one hour, claim it mine
and yours.

JANICE MOORE FULLER

Embrace me now
And let's hold one another
Until dawn.
Let's celebrate each other
With a poem,
Some lines
Stanzas of adoration

Must you hate me?
Yes, your skin is ivory
And mine is coal
Let's unite
And proclaim diversity
And be in awe of
The slanted Asian eyes
The pinkness of the Caucasian's face
The thickness of the Negro's lips

We all are one
For 60,000 pints of blood,
Collected on September 12 affirmed this.
Today I want to embrace you friend
And celebrate humankind
Until dawn

KEVIN DOUGLAS

## ⌒ PEACE ⌒

Ah, that Time could touch a form
That could show what Homer's age
Bred to be a hero's wage.
"Were not all her life but storm,
Would not painters paint a form
Of such noble lines," I said.
"Such a delicate high head,
So much sternness and such charm,
Till they had changed us to like strength?"
Ah, but peace that comes at length,
Came when Time had touched her form.

W. B. YEATS

## ⌒ DREAM OF SOULS RISING ⌒
### (after the World Trade Center attack)


Last night, after the towers fell, I lay down
on my bed and waited out the long dark
falling hours, the silent, falling shapes of death.

I slept, and in my dreams I heard a rattling cry
as if a horde of souls, escaped from hell,
clamored for re-entrance to the light.

And then I saw them, filling up the sky
horizon to horizon. Necks thrust out, voices
thrust before, they came and came from everywhere,

drawing my eye toward the far ends of the earth,
like a mind in search of full extension of a thought,
and climbing, swirled into a dark tumultuous

tunnel in the sky, the beating of their wings
a hard, determined, drumming noise, voices trumpets
summoning the laggard sleepers of the pit to rise.

So great their upward rush, the beating of their voice,
that stars plunged out of heaven, vanished in the sea,
till they at last burst through the swirling tunnel's

topmost gate, and rose and rose, and as they went,
dark necks stretched up into the light, dark sinewed
bodies became white and glowed like swans at dawn

and vanished up—yet still they came, and still.
And then I dreamed myself awake, and leaping
from my bed, flung up the blind, the window too,

saw them coming out of everywhere, just everywhere,
saw my soul leap out to them, and rise,
felt great rippling wings unfold.


JOANNA CATHERINE SCOTT

## HANDS

(In memory of the people who died on Sept. 11
and in hope that the living will one day find peace)


### The Question


The question concerns hands.
"God will pull your father up to heaven,"
a mother tells her small daughter after
terrorists crashed two passenger
planes into the twin towers of the
World Trade Center sending
thousands to their death.
The little girl asks:
"Does God have enough hands?"


### The Ground


That day when glass and steel
and many beating hearts collapsed,
some jumped together holding hands.
Workers found them still linked hand-in-hand
in death amongst the rubble; they found others'
hands tied behind their backs.

Men clutch edges of buckets and empty the gritty
contents already sifted for any trace of someone.
People search for their dear ones.
They clasp photographs and thrust them out to any
passersby hoping someone will have seen their
husbands, wives, fathers, mothers, sisters,
brothers, aunts, uncles, cousins, friends
alive.

They keep going beyond exhaustion.
"If I smile, I let him down.
If I sleep, I let him down," says one woman
looking for her brother.

Some escape thanks to helping hands.
Two men carry a woman in a wheelchair down
sixty-eight flights of stairs in one tower as stairwell
walls start to craze. It takes one hour.
They do not know her name.
A police officer tells of being buried
and how he saw a chink of light,
heard a voice telling him to grab onto
the hand extended through the murk
and he did, stretching his other hand back
to someone and that person to another
and so on and together, they followed
the light to safety.

The Memorial

Grief streams down the aisles,
wells up to stained glass windows
blackened by night in the crowded
cathedral at the memorial service
for all those lost, including the living.

Before the music starts, already a sense of peace,
a time to note how the fluted walls
rise like frozen hymns, a time to remember
that men placed each stone to make this structure
rise with easy grace to inhabit the heavens.

At the front of the chapel in pews along
the left arm of the cross-shaped interior,
only the single hand of a violinist is visible,
her bow rising and falling on great swells
of sound from many string musicians,
who play the adagio, stretched into an immense
vessel for sorrow, contained only by a thin,
taut, yet unbroken membrane, to hold
the unbearable if only for a few measures.

A rustle like the sound of a calm
sea surge on oyster-shells as
almost 400 singers take their places.
In the requiem, their voices reach
thunderous crescendos with a force
that cracks grief open and lets it rise
like each hair on the head,
leaving the body light,
pulling the lost home.

A few pews up, a boy of five or six
snuggles next to his grandmother.
She constantly strokes his cheek, his hair
as though her touch could will him to
live to manhood in this uncertain world,
and to create a time of comfort
for him to remember when her hands
are stilled, and perhaps to reassure herself
that he and she still live.


The Light


"Make of yourself a light,"
the Buddha said just before he died.
On the cathedral lawn, a constellation of people
hold candles, their illuminated faces like moons
from sun's reflection, so that no line
remains between ground and sky.
Stars, candles gleam like knots of silver
thread in a midnight velvet quilt.
They cup one hand around the candles
to shield their lights from any dark wind.


SUSAN BROILI

Pipers in the surf—
glittering at their ankles,
the bright summer sun.

End of the season:
just beyond the ocean's reach,
a clump of rose hips.

CAROLINE ROWE MARTENS

# THE DAY THE GINKGOES CRIED

DEDICATED TO CHARLIE AND JUDY LITEKY

Silent sentinels stand
Saluting as we enter
Five thousand mourners
Eight abreast
"Crossing the line"
Into Fort Benning

Marching in protest and resistance
To close the School of the Assassins*
We process with caskets and crosses
Crying "presente" as the name
Of each civilian killed by US
Is lifted to the heavens

The hillside, a blanket of golden leaves
Tears of sorrow as the ginkgoes remember
Those tortured and murdered
In Central America
Tears of joy as the ginkgoes attend to
The depth of our caring and commitment.

SAM R. HOPE

NOVEMBER 1999

*School of the Americas, Fort Benning, GA

11 September 2001

It is a bloodstained horizon
whispering laa illaha il-lallah
prelude to a balmy evening
that envelops our embrace
we stand reaching across
sands, waters, airs full of blood

in the flash of a distant storm
i see you standing on another shore
torn hijab
billowing towards an unnamed wind.

we both wear veils
blood stained
tear stained
enshrouding separate truths.

ii

misty morning
teardrops of dust
choke and stain lips
that do not move
will not utter.

It is a morning of shores
sea shadows that caress memory
of another time
another veil
another woman needing
reaching
lifting

iii

into your eyes i swam
searching for veils
to lift
to wrap
to pierce
dance with
veils that elude such mornings
veils that stain such lips
veils tearing like music

iv

it is the covering of spirit
not the body
my hijab your hijab
connecting interweaving crawling snaking binding
into a sky that will not bend.


JAKI SHELTON GREEN

I used to think it would begin with words,
aimed below rigid minds
and fanatical thoughts,
piercing the iciest of hearts.
The world would change
as exploding volcanoes
of religious intolerance,
political tugs-of-war,
and racial prejudices
would stop their spewing
and world-wide eruptions
would cease because the
words of peace were spoken
and all people listened.

But now, I realize the solution
has to begin with hands.
Hands need no translation.
To hold a weapon, bind wounds,
or connect one person to another,
it is the hands that pull us apart
or bring us back together.
We can focus on mouths or faces,
when the nightly news camera zooms.
But it is the hands I want to see —
the raised fist or the hand outstretched.
It is the hands
Where peace begins…

JUDY LEWIS HENCH

Like you, I have shed many tears;
Choked on the dust, and despaired
   of finding life;
Grieved with the families and friends
   left behind who will never find even
   the part of a body of which to moan—

Death without closure—

I see in my mind's eye again and again
   the picture of the helmeted firemen
      raising the Stars and Stripes,
And I think that photograph will live in history
   and art and sculpture as the photo from WWII
      of soldiers raising the American Flag
         at Iwo Jima—a turning point in the struggle
         of freedom versus repression.

I regret to say that I sometimes view my life as
   "one damned war after another"—

And now we know that men have found a new way
   to kill thousands of people at once,
      another milestone in history.

DAMN!

MITCHELL FORREST LYMAN©
11.01

I did not go to Nam.
My oldest brother was
an officer and gentleman.
We're blessed He "made it home"
to His Family. He paid dearly
for our freedom. I wish
I wrote to Him there.
I pray…someday He'll
forgive me and His other
siblings and His parents.
Not simply forget, forgive.
He must be a Holy Man.


He's still my hero.
He was always there for me.
Can I ever repay Him??
Possibly!
Unlike my country
Possibly
My children and His children
can just be…
Possibly
We can all
live through them.

I remember Him on His knees
with 12oz.Everlasts. I cold
cocked Him...Maybe,
maybe not.
I'm not certain anymore.
It was many years ago.

He must be a Holy Man.


TIMOTHY F CROWLEY
1992

DENNIS M. CROWLEY, JR.
DETACHMENT COMMANDER, OSI
DANANG, VIETNAM, 1967
AWARDED THE BRONZE STAR
FATHER, HUSBAND, SON, GRANDFATHER, UNCLE, BROTHER

Walked through an orange grove
& came upon 5 men in baseball
caps hooting & stomping

like punk rock gods while 2
indoctrinated roosters bloodied
each other with steel
spurs. Since wars began

old men have sent the young
away to die & we are both.
OK taxpayers those warlords

of the chickenyard. We're all
hardwired with the hot red rooster
light — that sends us out to die.
The men bag up the casualties

& smooth out the ground. Marching
bands are like cocaine — they make
dread ecstacy & war a kind of weather

to survive, a few lives shed
for Glory. Never what it really is —
that happens to you & me alone
just one time, lights out, forever..

DAVID T. MANNING

*James Hilden-Minton
adapted this closing hymn
in chant form from the
most well-known prayer
of St. Francis of Assisi.*

# Instrument of Peace